WALKS IN CALDERDALE

HILLSIDE GUIDES

WALKS
IN
CALDERDALE

by

Paul Hannon

HILLSIDE  PUBLICATIONS

HILLSIDE PUBLICATIONS
11 Nessfield Grove
Exley Head
Keighley
West Yorkshire
BD22 6NU

Cover illustration: Stoodley Pike from near
Withens Gate (Walks 14 and 16)
Page 1: Abel Cross, Crimsworth Dean (Walk 6)

ISBN   1 870141 03 2

Printed in Great Britain by
Carnmor Print and Design
95/97 London Road
Preston
Lancashire
PR1 4BA

INTRODUCTION

'South Pennines' is the generally accepted term for describing that part of the Pennine range lying between the Yorkshire Dales and the Peak District, and the area explored in these pages constitutes the very heart of these southern Pennines, the upper valley of Yorkshire's river Calder. This is an extremely well-defined and compact geographical unit, the moorland watersheds with neighbouring valleys in Yorkshire and Lancashire being the limit of our exploration. Only to the east, where the Calder leaves the high country for the larger industrial towns, must an arbitrary line be drawn. Since 1974 the title 'Calderdale' has been put to use in local government, with whose patch we coincide apart from the aforementioned lower third of the district, where the conurbations of Halifax, Sowerby Bridge, Brighouse and Elland can be found.

The area of this guide commences at the 'gateway' of Sowerby Bridge, where the district's two rivers, Calder and Ryburn merge. Upstream the Ryburn strikes southwards to Ripponden and the moors, while the main valley heads west to the upper dale's two towns of Hebden Bridge and Todmorden. On the way it absorbs the major side valleys carved out by Luddenden Brook, Cragg Brook, Hebden Water and Walsden Water.

The larger settlements squeeze sardine-like into the cramped valley floor, which is shared with river, canal, road and railway. Steep flanks rise in most cases to intervening ledges where older villages, predecessors of their bigger brothers below, almost shake hands across the deep divides. Higher still, rough pasture gives way to open moorland, where the mill chimney 2 miles away might as well be 200 miles distant. Calderdale's beauty is its unique blend of town and country: here the two are inextricably linked, and once one accepts the less appealing aspects of industrial demands, then one can revel in a feast of fascinating walking country.

Many features of this district's industrial past, in particular, provide much of interest to the observant walker. The hills hereabouts are laced with a centuries-old network of trading routes used mainly by packhorses: many of these escaped 'improvement', and numerous sections of stone causeway have survived, laying virtually dormant in wait for today's foot-traveller to bring them back to life, albeit for a new purpose. Hugging the valley bottom, in contrast, is the Rochdale Canal, which largely replaced the packhorse routes and whose towpath now provides miles of leisurely, uninterrupted walking.

Tumbling to the floor of the upper dale at regular

intervals are short-lived but deep-cut and richly wooded little valleys; these are cloughs, where some of the earliest mills were built in the most unlikely settings. Up on the tops one is never far from a reservoir, the earlier ones made to serve the canal, others to slake the ever-growing thirsts of the towns down the valley. This is definitive gritstone country, and sharing the higher ground with the reservoirs are numerous clusters of boulders and crags, the weathered natural outcrops outshining the countless sites of former quarries. Mainly small-scale operations, known as 'delphs', they provided material for the hoary drystone walls, reservoirs and buildings throughout the dale.

Interestingly enough the river Calder, underlying theme of these walks, is actually followed on only one of them, and even then more by accident than design as it happens to be parallel with the canal at that point. No, Calderdale's walking is not in the valley bottom, it is to be found on the hillsides and bracing tops of this characterful upland.

Self-proclaimed 'South Pennine Centre', Hebden Bridge is equally undeniably the focal point for this set of walks. It is for here that most of the modern 'tourists' make, partly for its position at the foot of the famous Hebden Dale (universally Hardcastle Crags), but also for its own attractions. Its houses climb alarmingly up the steep hillsides above the meeting of the valleys, while in and near the lively centre are canal trips, a packhorse bridge, clog factory, collectors' shops, the base of Pennine Heritage, and an invaluable information centre.

Near-neighbour Todmorden may have less obvious charm, but still provides great interest with its impressive Town Hall, spacious Centre Vale Park, and the gaunt Dobroyd Castle, once home of the mighty Fielden family, important mill owners and local benefactors. Unlike its counterparts in the valley, which thrived on the woollen industry, Todmorden and its mills were geared to the Lancashire cotton industry; indeed until a century ago Todmorden was quite literally on the border. Of the three roads heading out, two aim for the red rose towns of Rochdale and Burnley, both more accessible than Todmorden's Yorkshire masters: a hint of divided loyalties clearly remains hereabouts!

A particularly welcome aspect of walking in this well-populated district is the availability of public transport. Almost all of the starting points are served by buses, while a good rail service patrols the valley bottom. Such is the compactness of the area that two-thirds of the walks are within a couple of miles of a station. A general guide to the various facilities will be found overleaf.

The waymarking and condition of paths is very good overall, an indication of the local authority's highly commendable valuation of its outstanding path network. In our travels we encounter the Pennine Way, which crosses the area from Warland Reservoir in the south to Walshaw Dean in the north; and the Calderdale Way, a 50-mile path which encircles the district. The latter is a splendid example of what can be achieved in an 'unfashionable' area, and its popularity is a fitting tribute to the work involved in its creation. This too we encounter, on various occasions.

The 16 walks described vary from 3¾ to 7 miles, and all are circular. Each has its own chapter, comprising of 'immediate impression' diagram, detailed narrative and strip map, and notes and illustrations of features of interest.

While the strip-maps will guide one safely around, they cannot depict the surrounding countryside. Ordnance Survey maps are the obvious answer, and the 1:25,000 South Pennines Outdoor Leisure Map covers every walk. Conversely, the 1:50,000 Landranger Maps require 4 sheets, 103,104,109,110.

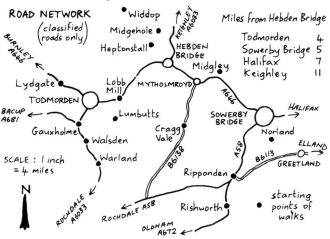

ROAD NETWORK
(classified)
roads only)

Miles from Hebden Bridge

Todmorden   4
Sowerby Bridge   5
Halifax   7
Keighley   11

SCALE : 1 inch = 4 miles

N

starting points of walks

7

SOME USEFUL FACILITIES

	Accommodation	Inn	Car Park	Bus service	Post Office	Shop	WC	Payphone
Baitings	✓	✓	✓	✓				
Colden	✓	✓		✓				✓
Cragg Vale	✓	✓		✓	✓		✓	✓
Gauxholme	✓	✓		✓	✓	✓		✓
Heptonstall	✓	✓	✓	✓	✓	✓	✓	✓
Lobb Mill			✓	✓				
Lumbutts		✓		✓				
Lydgate	✓	✓	✓	✓	✓	✓		✓
Mankinholes	✓			✓				
Midgehole			✓	✓			✓	✓
Midgley			✓		✓	✓		✓
Norland	✓	✓		✓			✓	✓
Pecket Well	✓	✓		✓				✓
Ripponden	✓	✓	✓	✓	✓	✓	✓	✓
Rishworth/Booth Wood	✓	✓	✓	✓	✓		✓	✓
Walsden	✓	✓	✓	✓	✓	✓		✓
Warland		✓		✓				
Widdop		✓		✓ (summer)				

Mankinholes has the only youth hostel (though Haworth is nearby).
All facilities (including railway stations) can be found at Hebden Bridge, Mytholmroyd, Sowerby Bridge and Todmorden.

SOME USEFUL ADDRESSES

The Ramblers' Association
    1/5 Wandsworth Road, London SW8 2XX
      Tel. 01 - 582 6878

Youth Hostels Association
    Trevelyan House, St.Albans, Herts AL1 2DY
      Tel. 0727 - 55215

Yorkshire and Humberside Tourist Board
    312 Tadcaster Road, York YO2 2HF
      Tel. 0904 - 707961

Tourist Information
    Piece Hall, Halifax, W.Yorkshire HX1 1RE
      Tel. 0422 - 68725

    1 Bridge Gate, Hebden Bridge, W.Yorks. HX7 8EX
      Tel. 0422 - 843831

    40 Town Hall St, Sowerby Bridge HX6 2AE
      Tel. 0422 - 835326

    15 Burnley Rd, Todmorden, Lancs. OL14 7BU
      Tel. 0706 - 818181

The National Trust (Regional Office)
    27 Tadcaster Road, York YO2 2QG
      Tel. 0904 - 702021

Yorkshire Rider (bus services)
    Skircoat Rd, Halifax HX1 2RF
      Tel. Bradford (0274) 720505

Pennine Heritage
    The Birchcliffe Centre, Hebden Bridge HX7 8DG
      Tel. 0422 - 844450

Calderdale Way Association
    Hon. Secretary: Miss M. Rooker
    16 Trenance Gardens, Greetland, Halifax HX4 8NN
      Tel. 0422 - 73832

THE WALKS

Listed below are the 16 walks described, the walk number being the key to easy location in the guide

THE WALKS

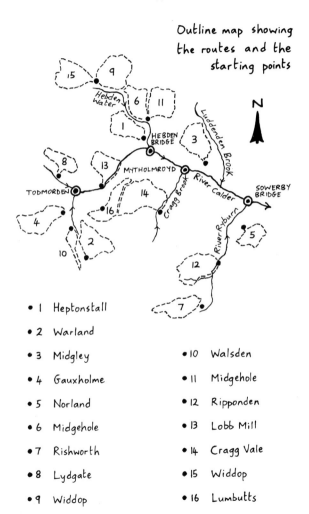

Outline map showing
the routes and the
starting points

N

- 1   Heptonstall
- 2   Warland
- 3   Midgley
- 4   Gauxholme
- 5   Norland
- 6   Midgehole
- 7   Rishworth
- 8   Lydgate
- 9   Widdop
- 10   Walsden
- 11   Midgehole
- 12   Ripponden
- 13   Lobb Mill
- 14   Cragg Vale
- 15   Widdop
- 16   Lumbutts

WALK 1

5½ miles

ABOVE COLDEN AND HEBDEN WATERS

from Heptonstall

A splendid promenade
above two deep
wooded valleys,
and free
of any
noticeable
gradients.
A wedge
of heather
moorland
divides
the two
legs.

Start from Heptonstall
car park.

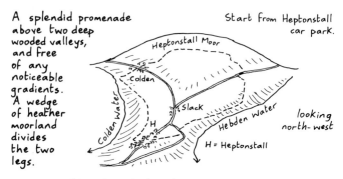

looking
north-west

H = Heptonstall

Alternative start: National Trust car park at Clough
Hole on the Heptonstall-Widdop road *(see map).*

THE WALK

From the car park re-enter the main street and turn
uphill. Beyond the two inns take the first turn right along
Townfield Lane, continuing past the last of the houses as a
walled green lane. When the left-hand wall ceases at a stile,
strike half-left across the field to join a road, then head
left a short distance to a stile in the opposite wall. From
here a footpath commences a generally level course above the
wooded slopes of Hebden Dale.

At a natural viewing platform just beyond a former
quarry (take care here) turn up an enclosed path, leaving it
immediately by a stile on the right. Across a field-bottom our
original route resumes along the wood-top, though soon the
path begins a steady descent through the trees. Continuing
at mid-height a wide track is joined at a hairpin bend, and
is followed with ease uphill to leave the trees and rise up to
the road at Clough Hole.

Turn right past the car park entrance then at once
head up the drive to Clough House. Pass in front of the farm
buildings to a gate, behind which is a wet track between a
brace of crumbling walls, which soon swings right to head up
the field in sunken fashion. The crumbling walls return as

12

derelict Clough Head appears above, and two stiles in quick succession lead to it. Go left past the ruin to a gap in the wall corner, and follow a path away with a wall towards a gateway above a beck crossing: just in front is a cairn marking our arrival on the Pennine Way.

While the main path strikes across the moor, a drier alternative accompanies the wall left, then climbs the moorside on a narrower path to regain the Pennine Way on the brow. It goes on to a small gate in the far left corner by a lone house, and dropping down, the nearby walls soon close in tightly to usher the path onto a narrow road. A few yards to the right the path continues down a field-side to a wider road. Go straight across and down to Goose Hey farm, turning left of it through two small gates and diagonally across a pasture on a flagged path to a stile.

A walled path now descends to Colden Water, with a fork just above the beck. Here the Pennine Way is left in favour of a better flagged path along to the left, running between the fields and the drop to the beck. On entering trees a stile is met at a kink in the accompanying wall, and here the stone causeway vacates the environs of the beck to cross several fields before losing its solid surface. A good path goes on to soon become enclosed before merging with a similar way to rise to a T-junction.

Take the track right, passing behind a barn to a stile whereupon a further paved section leads to yet another enclosed track. Turn down it to join a narrow access road and head up this until a path strikes off to the right. A grand level walk ensues high above Colden Water, soon opening out and remaining with the left-hand wall until an enclosed path strikes reluctantly off to the left, beckoned by the tower of Heptonstall church. At a fork before the church, either of its two branches will lead back onto the main street.

Heptonstall is a fascinating village that well merits an hour's leisurely exploration. Steeped in history, it was of greater importance than Hebden Bridge until the arrival of the Industrial Revolution. Happily its exposed position 850 feet up and defended on three sides by precipitous slopes has created a time warp in which its weatherbeaten stone cottages revel. Focal point is the churchyard which separates the imposing parish church of 1854 from the shell of the old church of St. Thomas a' Becket, partly dating from the 13th century. Alongside is the museum, a former grammar school of 1772; seek out also the octagonal Wesleyan chapel (1764), the old dungeon (1824) and the 16th century Cloth Hall.

Hebble Hole Bridge is a characterful, ancient footbridge consisting of two great stone slabs. This charming location merits the few yards' detour. Here the Pennine and Calderdale Ways have one of their two meetings.

Clough Hole falls can be seen with a short scramble down the bank just before leaving the woods. A splendid series of cataracts continue down to the bottom.

This early cotton mill is seen from our path above. Walk 6 passes it in the valley of Hebden Water, better known as Hardcastle Crags. Our walk above Hebden Wood boasts glorious views over the richly wooded valley.

The final section above Eaves Wood reveals dramatic views from gritstone outcrops down the steep heather and bilberry clad slopes into Colden Clough. Particularly grand is Stoodley Pike, seen from valley floor to the towering monument.

Map labels:

Clough Head (ruin)
Heptonstall Moor
Clough House
WIDDOP
Clough Hole Falls
③
1200'
SLACK
②
Gibson Mill
Hebden Water
Mount Pleasant
BLACKSHAW HEAD
Colden
MYTHOLM
Goose Hey (farm)
tiny housing estate
④
Hebble Hole Bridge
Colden Water
Hebden Wood
COLDEN
①
Lee Bank
HEBDEN BRIDGE
⑤
COLDEN
Eaves Wood
immediate views over to Hardcastle Crags
car park
Heptonstall
HEBDEN BRIDGE
N

Waterfall, Clough Hole

'Heptonstall History Trail' by Calder Civic Trust is obtainable locally.

The ruin of
St. Thomas
a' Becket,
Heptonstall

Stoodley Pike
and the
Calder valley
from above
Eaves Wood,
Heptonstall

WALK 2

6½ miles

SALTER RAKE AND WALSDEN MOOR

from Warland

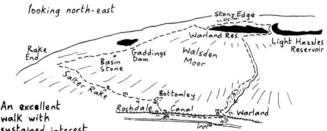

looking north-east

An excellent
walk with
sustained interest
from towpath to moor
top, and easy to follow
paths, to boot.

Start from the Bird i'th' Hand inn, near to
the county boundary (Grid ref. 944201). Verge
parking besides the inn's patrons' car park.

THE WALK

From the Bird i'th' Hand inn cross the road and take
the rough lane (Warland Gate End) heading away to cross the
Rochdale Canal. Between two houses it starts a long climb to
the moor, becoming surfaced at a sharp bend to rise up to a
waterworks building and a lone house. Follow the track up past
the red brick building to a derelict farm just above, passing along
its front and up to a gate to its right. A track continues up the
moor to a gate in a fence above, to then rise in harmony with
the adjacent beck.

As the grassy retaining wall of Warland Reservoir is
approached, either take the steeper left-hand path to the top,
or follow the wide track right to the southern extremity of the
reservoir. Here leave the water board road and strike off on a
path along the embankment of neighbouring Light Hazzles. At
its far end the path swings left, still on a distinct embankment
of a defunct catchwater. Nearing the shore of Warland Reservoir
again we pass below the boulders of Stony Edge before gaining
the reservoir road again, now at the reservoir's northernmost
point.

Cross the concrete drain and follow it to the right,
only as far as a sharp bend; here strike off left across the
moor on a path in the direction of Gaddings Dam. A little
wet in parts, it skirts a miniature boulder field to traverse

the left-hand embankment of the reservoir. Below a flight of steps the path continues down the moor, past the Basin Stone and trending right towards Todmorden in the valley bottom.

A little over half a mile beyond Gaddings Dam look out for a crossroads with a part-paved way, this being the Salter Rake: it is not at its most distinct as we turn to the left along it, just prior to its rounding Rake End, on our right. The path slopes down across the moor, taking in an easily by-passed marshy section before entering walled confines at North Hollingworth. When the access road turns right continue straight on along a drive to South Hollingworth.

From a gate beneath the house ignore the wide track up the field and instead trace the sketchy causeway along the field bottom. At the next gate it descends to the back of Dean Royd, then rises left again to a footbridge over a tiny beck. Across it the hamlet of Bottomley is entered: turn right and at a gate a superb cobbled way descends to the Rochdale Canal again at Bottomley Lock. Go left along the towpath to return to Warland, finishing along Warland Gate End to rejoin the main road.

Stony Edge from the old drain, Warland Reservoir

~ Winter on Walsden Moor ~

The Basin Stone, looking to Reddyshore Scout

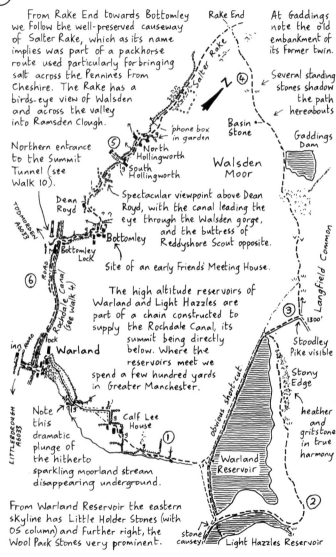

From Rake End towards Bottomley we follow the well-preserved causeway of Salter Rake, which as its name implies was part of a packhorse route used particularly for bringing salt across the Pennines from Cheshire. The Rake has a birds-eye view of Walsden and across the valley into Ramsden Clough.

Northern entrance to the Summit Tunnel (see Walk 10).

Spectacular viewpoint above Dean Royd, with the canal leading the eye through the Walsden gorge, and the buttress of Reddyshore Scout opposite.

Site of an early Friends' Meeting House.

The high altitude reservoirs of Warland and Light Hazzles are part of a chain constructed to supply the Rochdale Canal, its summit being directly below. Where the reservoirs meet we spend a few hundred yards in Greater Manchester.

Note this dramatic plunge of the hitherto sparkling moorland stream disappearing underground.

From Warland Reservoir the eastern skyline has Little Holder Stones (with OS column) and further right, the Wool Pack Stones very prominent.

At Gaddings note the old embankment of its former twin.

Several standing stones shadow the path hereabouts

Map labels:

Rake End

Salter Rake

phone box in garden

North Hollingworth

South Hollingworth

Basin Stone

Walsden Moor

Gaddings Dam

Dean Royd

TODMORDEN A6033

Bottomley

Bottomley Lock

Rochdale Canal (see Walk 4)

ROAD

lock

Warland

in road

Langfield Common

Stoodley Pike visible

Stony Edge

heather and gritstone in true harmony

1300'

obvious short-cut

Calf Lee House

LITTLEBROUGH A6033

Warland Reservoir

stone causey

Light Hazzles Reservoir

18

WALK 3

MIDGLEY MOOR AND LUDDENDEN DEAN

6¼ miles

from Midgley

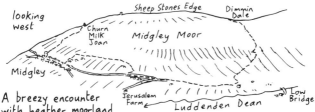

looking west

Sheep Stones Edge

Dimmin Dale

Churn Milk Joan

Midgley Moor

Midgley

Jerusalem Farm

Luddenden Dean

Low Bridge

A breezy encounter
with heather moorland
and a simple stroll down
a well-wooded valley.

Start from the village centre
(thoughtful roadside parking needed).

Alternative start: Jerusalem Farm, Luddenden (limited parking - see map).

THE WALK

Follow the road through the village from the inn to the western end, and just before a fork in the road turn up Chapel Lane. Past the Methodist church the lane turns grassy as it rises to the left between two houses. Beyond a gate continue up to the left on the top side of a sunken way, and from a stile in an intervening fence rise over the open moor to meet the level course of the Calderdale Way.

Go left with this path which soon begins a steady rise up to a prominent wall-corner, with the even more conspicuous boundary stone of Churn Milk Joan a few yards higher on the skyline. Here turn left on the wide wallside path until the wall turns sharply left. Here take the path going half-left across the moor, bearing right on nearing a moor edge fence. A good path runs parallel with the fence before taking a stile in it to drop down a little towards the building (a clubhouse) below. Remaining on the moor the wide path contours round above the golf course and below old quarries in a great loop below Cock Hill, then heads north with the intake wall/fence.

A superb path now takes us along the moor bottom, and is only vacated when it turns sharp left with the intake: here a cairn signifies the presence of a junction, from where a narrower path heads sharp right up the moor. After a short climb it levels out to run alongside a row of shooting butts crossing the ridge in the depression known as Dimmin Dale.

The path by the butts soon drops down towards the Luddenden Dean side of the moor, bearing right to a crumbling wall corner at the well defined moor edge. While a thin path runs along the edge, ours begins to descend, doubling back briefly to the wall before a well graded slope down to the right. It becomes a little wet and sketchy before a gate just above Goose Green, from where a splendid green lane leads down to a broad access lane. Turn right along it, emerging, after a short mile, at a junction with a hairpin bend.

Head up the road to the right, ignoring a 'no through road' a little higher and continuing along the lane which has a brief unsurfaced spell before climbing again to a junction. Here turn right a few yards and then left up a farm drive. On approaching the farm take a stile on the right to regain the heather of Midgley Moor, and the Calderdale Way again.

An excellent path runs above the wall, all too soon reaching a stile when a fence takes over. Here drop down to two houses, go right a few yards along the drive, then right again through a gate at a drive 'junction'. When it rises to a farm in the second field, keep straight on by the wall to a slim gapstile in it. Descend a field to pass right of a row of cottages at Scotland, and continue down a surprising flagged path through the last field to Tray Royd. Its flagged drive then descends to the road by the inn in the village.

Churn Milk Joan, looking to Stoodley Pike

Luddenden Dean is a gracefully curving valley born on the high moors and running a deep course down to the parent valley. We enter the dale at the start of a private drive heading updale to the grounds and abandoned house of Castle Carr, immediately beneath two reservoirs.

The village of Midgley clings to the hillside, its houses strung out along its 'main street'. Note the stocks.

Sudden view updale over Hebden Bridge and Heptonstall on arriving above the clubhouse of Mount Skip golf club.

Churn Milk Joan is a sturdy six feet high boundary stone.

The monument on Stoodley Pike appears at the very outset of the walk. To its left the deep trough of Cragg Vale strikes into the heart of the moors southwards.

Superb views into Luddenden Dean from the moor edge here. Both reservoirs are visible up the valley.

Midgley Moor is an extensive heather tract much enjoyed by grouse until August.

Early in the walk we have an impressive birds-eye view of the uninspiring environs of Mytholmroyd.

✳ ─ ✳ Map extended to show easier route remaining on the moor in the event of a start from Jerusalem.

Tray Royd is a most characterful residence, clearly of some age.

Midgley

21

WALK 4

6½ miles

from Gauxholme

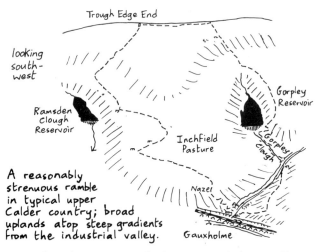

A reasonably
strenuous ramble
in typical upper
Calder country; broad
uplands atop steep gradients
from the industrial valley.

Start from the junction of the A6033 and the A681 Bacup
road, a short mile south of Todmorden centre. A long, low
railway viaduct straddles the junction. There is roadside
parking (limited) where the Bacup road crosses the canal.

THE WALK

From the road bridge over the canal head away from
the viaduct and turn left almost at once along the apparently
short-lived Naze Road. This inauspicious start soon perks up at a
gate on the left at the end of the tripeworks yard, for at once
the grime is traded for a broad green track. Doubling back almost
immediately, a steep climb of the Naze ensues, made easy by the
series of zig-zags. As the gradient eases the climb continues 'twixt
old walls to a stile, from where a short enclosed section takes
us onto the open moor. Go forward to join a wide track, but
when it bears left at a wall-corner take the lesser fork straight
ahead, to trace a stone causey across the otherwise soggy
moorland of Inchfield Pasture.

Beyond a beck crossing the path deteriorates, but keep

22

straight on, going left of a pond to join the broad unsurfaced Foul Clough Road by Thorns Greece farm. Turn right along it, sweeping around above the intake wall to a stile and gate just above the last house. The track continues between crumbling walls to a fork: take the right one to resume the climb, by and then over a lively beck to pass near a sombre ruin to a gate in a fence. A stile just behind it gives access onto the moor beyond, and a damp track rises then swings right to the conspicuous site of an old mine. Here take a narrow trod rising behind: during its short, steep climb on easy grass it pulls half-right to impressively gain the Ordnance Survey column on Trough Edge End.

From the top cross the adjacent stile and go left with the fence to a junction, there turning right with the fence and old wall along the broad ridge top. As the fence parts company keep straight on, a rather exceptional wall is soon to take its place. When this wall ends a boggy pool will be seen over the replacement wall. Only 40 yards beyond it a stile is reached: do not use it, but instead depart the ridge by descending directly away across surprisingly dry grass to join an old mine road at some former workings.

Cross straight over and continue down to the obvious head of a deep clough, trending left towards a collapsed wall rising away. On gaining the wall follow it up to the left and then away as it skirts the pronounced drop to Gorpley Reservoir. A fence soon takes over and the pathless march continues until a farm track emerges out of a field. This pleasant way improves progress no end, and soon drops down to an old farmyard. Go left between the buildings and out along the drive to a T-junction. Here turn right down the lane to the treatment plant below the dam of the reservoir.

After a semi-circle alongside the plant take a gate on the left to descend a flight of steps into wooded Gorpley Clough. The path through the length of the clough has had a complete restoration and is followed unerringly down, crossing and recrossing the beck to eventually emerge onto the A681 Bacup road. Turn right a short way then escape at a gap on the left beyond a house, on a path rising through Stones Wood.

At a kissing-gate it leaves the wood to cross two fields to a junction of green ways: rise left between walls, and at the top turn right to cross a field bottom. From a stile at the end go on past stables, then right through a gate to the front of a house. Pass along its front to detect a small gate onto an equally miniscule green way. It meets a steep track dramatically perched above the valley: turn down it to return to the start.

Waterfall,
Gorpley
Clough

Gorpley Clough is a charming wooded dell beneath
the reservoir, with a tinkling beck
enjoying two enchanting
moments, the lower cascade
being especially delectable.
A recent restoration of
the path has involved
phenomenal effort, and
though a little
artificial it
remains a
joy to tread.

The county
boundary
with Lancashire
occupies our broad
ridge north-west of
Trough Edge End.

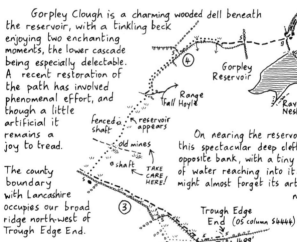

On nearing the reservoir note
this spectacular deep cleft on its
opposite bank, with a tiny finger
of water reaching into it. One
might almost forget its artificial
nature.

Trough Edge End is the
highest altitude attained in
these Calderdale walks, and is, hardly
surprisingly, an extensive viewpoint. Its
panorama is very much an upland one:
higher landmarks occupy the Pennine watershed to
north and south in the shape of Black Hameldon and
Blackstone Edge respectively, while to the east is (inevitably) Stoodley
Pike, and westwards the industry-ravaged moors of Rossendale.

Trough Edge End
Gorpley Reservoir

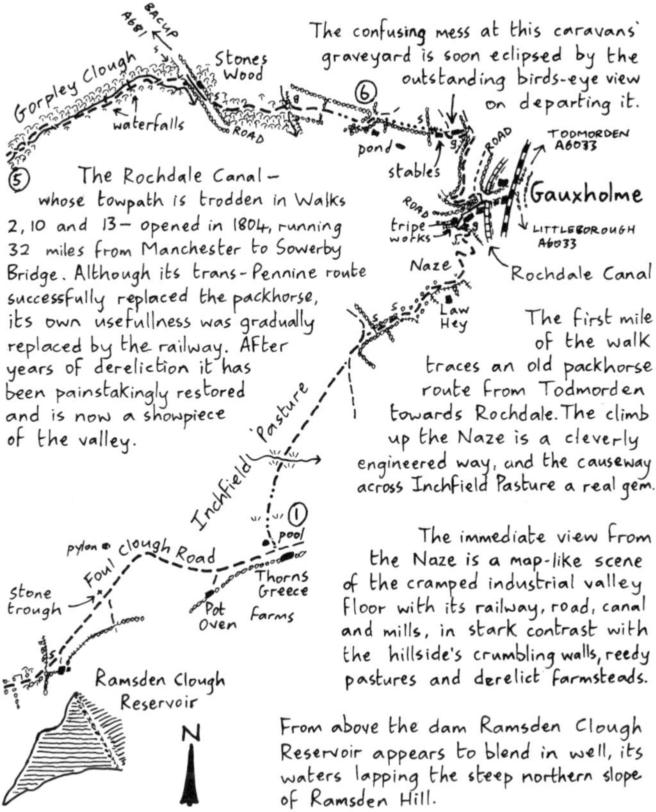

The confusing mess at this caravans' graveyard is soon eclipsed by the outstanding birds-eye view on departing it.

⑤ **The Rochdale Canal** — whose towpath is trodden in Walks 2, 10 and 13 — opened in 1804, running 32 miles from Manchester to Sowerby Bridge. Although its trans-Pennine route successfully replaced the packhorse, its own usefullness was gradually replaced by the railway. After years of dereliction it has been painstakingly restored and is now a showpiece of the valley.

The first mile of the walk traces an old packhorse route from Todmorden towards Rochdale. The climb up the Naze is a cleverly engineered way, and the causeway across Inchfield Pasture a real gem.

The immediate view from the Naze is a map-like scene of the cramped industrial valley floor with its railway, road, canal and mills, in stark contrast with the hillside's crumbling walls, reedy pastures and derelict farmsteads.

From above the dam Ramsden Clough Reservoir appears to blend in well, its waters lapping the steep northern slope of Ramsden Hill.

Map labels: Gorpley Clough, A681, BACUP, Stones Wood, waterfalls, ROAD, pond, stables, ROAD, TODMORDEN A6033, Gauxholme, tripe works, LITTLEBOROUGH A6033, Rochdale Canal, Naze, Law Hey, Inchfield Pasture, pylon, Foul Clough Road, pool, Stone trough, Thorns Greece Farms, Pot Oven, Ramsden Clough Reservoir, ① N

25

WALK 5

3¾ miles

An easy stroll round a
popular local
haunt. Ideal
for when time
is at a
premium.

| AROUND NORLAND MOOR |

from Norland

looking south-east

Start from the Moorcock Inn,
1 mile south-west of Norland on the
moor-bottom road to the B6113. Grid reference: 054218.
Ample roadside parking, as well as the inn's patrons' car park.
Alternative start: the Spring Rock Inn, 1 mile west of Greetland on B6113.

THE WALK

From the Moorcock take the broad track rising up
onto the moor to the former quarry of Turgate Delph, turning
right at the first opportunity on a good path along the well
defined edge. At the outcrop of Ladstone Rock a wider path is
joined and followed to the right to drop down towards a road.
Without having to set foot on it however, turn left across the
moor, picking up a sketchy path rising to the wall at the top.
Go left a few yards along a track, and at the wall's demise
turn right on a track by a fence and old wall. It is followed
its entire length, becoming enclosed on leaving the moor and
eventually emerging at the Spring Rock Inn.

Turn left along the road but then leave the main
road at once in favour of the Norland road to the left. Leave
this road just after a bend to follow a wall on the right of
a small uncultivated tract. At the end take the left-hand
of two stiles into a field, and trend slightly left aiming for
a conspicuous gap-stile in the wall ahead. Beyond it a wallside
is followed away to join a road with a pavement. Go left to a
junction, across which a broad path rises back onto the moor.

Amidst a labrynth of paths and tracks take the same
path directly over Norland Moor beneath a row of pylons to
eventually meet a wider track near the moor's westerly
escarpment. Go left along this track as it rises steadily across
the moor top, and on reaching the hollow of Turgate Delph
a return to the Moorcock can be made.

Ordnance column, looking to
Ladstone Rock

The Ladstone Rock

The natural gritstone outcrop of Ladstone Rock, a distinctive landmark, bears a God-praising plaque in the same 'series' as that in the beck at Gibson Mill, Hardcastle Crags (Walk 6).

Immediately north of the moor the sprawl of Halifax dominates, with the nearby Wainhouse Tower completely dwarfing the many mill chimneys and church spires.

Norland Town is an isolated hilltop settlement boasting some rather splendid clothiers' houses of centuries past.

Norland Moor is an island-like heather tract perched high above Sowerby Bridge and the Ryburn valley. Publicly owned for over half a century, it bears the much healed scars of extensive small-scale quarrying, notably along the western escarpment. The Ordnance column is not quite the loftiest point, although the ominous sounding Gallows Pole Hill, a third of a mile to the south, still doesn't demand a 1000 foot contour.

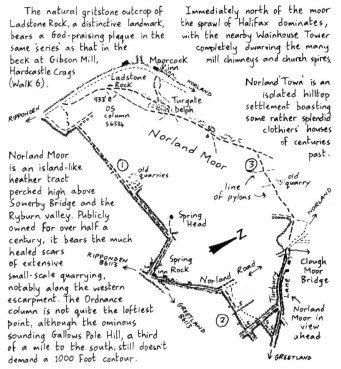

27

WALK 6

5¼ miles

| HARDCASTLE CRAGS AND ABEL CROSS |

from Midgehole

The renowned
woodlands of
Hardcastle Crags
are more than
ably supported by
a fine mooredge
track and a simple
stroll above the
colourful valley of
Crimsworth Dean.
Weekends usually
see sizeable crowds
at Hardcastle Crags.

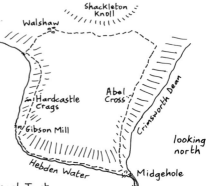

Start from the National Trust
car park at Midgehole. This (with overflow
facilities) is the main car park for Hardcastle Crags, signposted
off the Keighley road out of Hebden Bridge.

| THE WALK |

From the car park head up the drive a few yards
until just past the solitary Lodge, then fork left on a path
descending to Hebden Water. Here a wide beckside path is
met, and this is accompanied upstream for almost a mile
and a half, rarely straying far from the bank until the
imposing Gibson Mill is reached. Here the drive is rejoined
to climb above the beck, levelling out alongside the steep
rise of Hardcastle Crags themselves, just a brief scramble
up to the left.

Continuing on from the clearing by the Crags, a
left fork is soon taken to regain sight of the beck, the
wide path gradually declining towards it. After crossing
a side beck a minor crossroads is reached: the left branch
doubles back to a footbridge, while our route follows the
narrow path through a gateway on the right and climbs
steeply above the side beck. At the wood-top go left a
few yards to a small gate into a field, then rise to the
impressive front of Walshaw shooting lodge.

Just to the right of Walshaw shooting lodge a tiny enclosure is entered by a gate and left by a stile. Head up the yard and turn sharp right along its drive for a few yards before taking a gate on the left. From it a walled track heads away, soon becoming unenclosed and, after crossing a tiny beck, rising round the top side of a large pasture. Almost at the top corner a gate transfers us onto the moor proper, and a wide wallside track then contours round to the right beneath Shackleton Knoll.

As the environs of Crimsworth Dean are entered, the moor is vacated at a gate from where an enclosed track descends to a T-junction. Here turn right along a broader track which runs near-parallel with Crimsworth Dean Beck down to the left. This very track returns us unfailingly to Midgehole, with the only interruption being a diversion to inspect Abel Cross.

The way to Abel Cross is found just beyond a cattle-grid after the first farm buildings, where a stile lurks in the low wall on the right. Contour across the field to join a farm drive, with the two prominent shafts of Abel Cross just ahead. From here the main track is regained to enter woodland and continue a long, gradual descent back to the starting point of the walk.

Stepping stones, Hebden Hey

Hardcastle Crags

Hardcastle Crags is the name by which everyone in the district fondly knows the valley of Hebden Dale, through which flows Hebden Water. The majority of this beautifully-wooded, deep-cut dale is in the care of the National Trust, and attracts large crowds from far and wide. The 'Crags' themselves are a group of modest outcrops on a prominent knoll, with a tiny ridge rising well above the tree tops. As a result this airy spot is a superb vantage point, a place to linger.

This farm above us bears the delightful name of Horodiddle →

Walshaw

an ancient settlement

Shackleton Knoll

③

1215'

highest point

Coppy Lane

ruin

Nook (ruin)

From Walshaw to the foot of Coppy Lane we follow a route used in the 17th century to transport lime from Lancashire to Calder valley farms.

Laithe

④

Abel Cross

Abel Cross is in fact two identical crosses, thought to mark a medieval packway route.

Crimsworth Dean is seen in more detail during Walk 11.

Hebden Water

②

Hardcastle Crags

Gibson Mill was founded in 1800 as an early waterpowered cotton mill. After enlargement it ceased to operate in the 1890's, becoming a curiously-sited dance hall and even a roller-skating rink. The building still remains intact - with some related features nearby - and is an imposing sight in its wooded environs.

Crimsworth Dean Beck

wooden shelter

Gibson Mill

Tablet affixed to rock in beck, giving praise to God.

①

⑤

N

Hebden Hey

※ = stepping stones

Horse Bridge

HEBDEN BRIDGE

The rapid transition from rich woodland to the bleak moorland above Walshaw is quite remarkable. Ubiquitous features of the view are Heptonstall church and distant Stoodley Pike monument.

Hebden Water

Midgehole

WALK 7

5¼ miles

| RISHWORTH MOOR AND BOOTH DEAN |

from Rishworth

An invigorating ramble over archetypal
Pennine moorland.

looking north

Start from the A672 Oldham road where
it gains the open moor, half a mile west of the Turnpike inn,
Grid reference 019161. (Further parking available along the moor road).
Alternative start: roadside parking area at Booth Wood Reservoir's dam,
further east (1½ miles out of Rishworth). An extra mile's walking involved.

‖ NB: this walk is largely over open country, and it is suggested the
‖ nearest we get to a 'settled' day be chosen. Don't be put off now!

| THE WALK |

Almost immediately after emerging onto Rishworth Moor
the A672 passes defunct quarries on either side. Immediately
after the more striking left-hand one a guidepost indicates a
footpath branching off to the left. Though narrow, it quickly
becomes clear to follow a near-level course along the narrow
piece of moor between the road above and the various waters
of Booth Dean below. Beyond the last reservoir the path soon
rises to the road at Oxygrains Bridge, dwarfing the old bridge
at the confluence below.

Cross the road (but not the bridge) and head up the
valley of Oxygrains on a splendid green path running along
to the rugged environs of Castle Dean Rocks. Rising above the
rocks the path swings round with the beck to see the dam of
Green Withens Reservoir high in front. Occasionally sketchy, the
path heads for the dam, rising to the right on nearing it to
emerge at its northern end. Turn right along the reservoir road,
which then swings sharp right to follow the wide drain away.

Becoming a rougher track, the drain-side road is left

by crossing the fourth bridge since joining it. The path rises half-right over the moor, faltering at a beck crossing with a miniscule stone 'dam'. Continue by rising slightly to the head of another tiny beck, then aim for the conspicuous sunken track at Whinny Nick on the skyline just ahead. From here the view eastward opens up, and it is this direction we take, by keeping higher ground to the left and following a distinct grass strip, descending imperceptibly between groughs above and wetter terrain below.

Before too long we merge with a better defined grassy track from the right, continuing on to pass through a rash of stones from where a reedy ditch accompanies us. Soon the track forks right, but our way remains with the ditch: a little further the ditch appears to fork, and a waymark on a prominent boulder confirms that left is the way to go. The slopes to the left have diminished to the extent that there is a wide view to the north, and no uphill work is needed to gain the north side of this broad moorland tongue. At the well-defined Blackwood Edge this sunken way and a materialising path turn right, running above the steeper drop to a tall ladder-stile in an intervening wall.

Without crossing the stile turn right on a part-sunken path crossing the brow of the moor to a gate in a facing wall. Descend a field to stiles right of a barn then join its drive to go down to a sharp bend. To return to Booth Wood dam go left (see map), otherwise use the Kissing-gate on the right from where a wide track heads away to finish, appropriately, back on the moor, joining the road at the old quarries where the walk began.

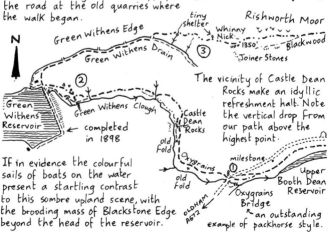

The vicinity of Castle Dean Rocks make an idyllic refreshment halt. Note the vertical drop from our path above the highest point.

Oxygrains Bridge — an outstanding example of packhorse style.

If in evidence the colourful sails of boats on the water present a startling contrast to this sombre upland scene, with the brooding mass of Blackstone Edge beyond the head of the reservoir.

32

Oxygrains
Old Bridge

Apart from the final mile, all the walking is on the urban common of Rishworth Moor, its value rightly extolled by the local authority.

From Blackwood Edge there are extensive views north over the upper Ryburn valley.

Blackwood Edge 'Road' originally serviced the moorland quarries.

Immediately south of Booth Dean the M62 motorway climbs to its summit at Windy Hill, where a mast tops the skyline. Ideally one acquires immunity against the constant drone of traffic.

Blackwood Edge

old quarry

boulder ④

Edge Road

N

These lush green pastures are quite a culture shock after the miles of rough moorland.

Inscribed milestone in wall
(Rochdale/Halifax/ Huddersfield)

Boan (barn)

RISHWORTH A672

Booth Wood

Rishworth Lodge

The wonderful path through Booth Dean and Oxygrains traces the course of a 2 mile long railway line constructed to convey stone for the building of Green Withens Reservoir.

⑤

old quarries

950'

Turnpike inn

Booth Wood Reservoir

Lower Booth Dean Reservoir

Compare the happy tinkling of this beck over gritstone slabs with the regular adjacent outflow over concrete.

‖ The map has been extended to the dam of Booth Wood Reservoir to include a longer approach from its car park. With its mighty dam the 50 acre reservoir was completed in 1971, fifty years after its similarly slender and attractive little neighbours upstream.

WALK 8
6¼ miles

WHIRLAW AND THE BRIDE STONES
from Lydgate

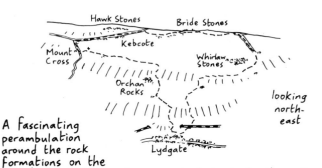

A fascinating
perambulation
around the rock
formations on the
hillside above Todmorden.

Lydgate is 1¼ miles north-west of Todmorden on the
Burnley road. There is street parking in the vicinity of the
Post office, and a large millside car park nearer Todmorden
centre (see map). Grid ref (Lydgate Post office) 923255.

THE WALK

Leave the main road (A646) by Church Road next
to the Post office, and at the end bear right on a private
looking drive. An enclosed footpath materialises, passing to
the right of the last house and emerging at an immense
railway arch. Head underneath it on a drive which rises
past Stannally, through trees and then a wicket gate onto
the open country of Stannally Stones. Here it swings right to
approach a farm, passing left of the buildings for us to
follow a sunken way up to a walled track.

Turn right along the track, soon emerging to cross
a damp pasture on flags to reach Whirlaw Common. The
path runs beneath Whirlaw Stones, remaining flagged until
becoming enclosed again. Within a few yards escape by a
gap on the left as a stream comes in, and rise to join a
wall climbing the slope. A little left of the wall a track
materialises and rises to a gapstile at the top right-hand
corner.

The terminus of Windy Harbour Lane is joined, and

after an initial pull it runs along to meet Eastwood Road. Go left only as far as the end of the left-hand wall, to then cross a hurdle from where a sinuous path makes its way across Bride Stones Moor to the prominent outcrops of the same name. On traversing the stones the path fades, but simply continue on to a further cluster of outcrops immediately above Bride Stones farm.

From there bear right along a broken fence along the line of the stones, a track soon coming in to guide us to a stile onto an access track beyond the last rocks. Turn right onto a road and then left along it for an easy mile as far as a junction. Turn down to the left and at the first opportunity go left on a walled track opposite a farm on the right.

This old route is the one encountered during the approach to Whirlaw, and its near-level course is followed in that direction. Almost immediately a glance over the upper wall will reveal Mount Cross. After about a mile, at the brow beyond a bridge over Redmires Water, take a stile on the right and follow a track by the wallside down past the flat-topped Orchan Rocks.

Below the rocks the track goes through a gate and down to a junction: double back to the left here, dropping further to become enclosed. This same track now takes us all the way down, largely through trees, to the valley bottom. As civilisation is embraced turn left at the first houses to a steep drop onto the side street on which the walk commenced.

Bride Stones   Mount Cross   Whirlaw

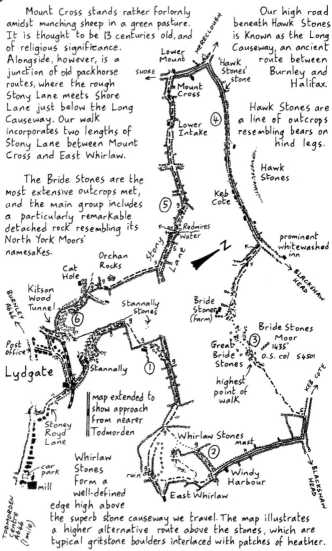

Mount Cross stands rather forlornly amidst munching sheep in a green pasture. It is thought to be 13 centuries old, and of religious significance. Alongside, however, is a junction of old packhorse routes, where the rough Stony Lane meets Shore Lane just below the Long Causeway. Our walk incorporates two lengths of Stony Lane between Mount Cross and East Whirlaw.

The Bride Stones are the most extensive outcrops met, and the main group includes a particularly remarkable detached rock resembling its North York Moors' namesakes.

Our high road beneath Hawk Stones is known as the Long Causeway, an ancient route between Burnley and Halifax.

Hawk Stones are a line of outcrops resembling bears on hind legs.

MERECLOUGH

Lower Mount

SHORE

'Hawk Stones' stone

Mount Cross

④

Lower Intake

Hawk Stones

Keb Cote

⑤

Stony Lane

Redmires Water

N

prominent whitewashed inn

BLACKSHAW HEAD

Orchan Rocks

Cat Hole

Kitson Wood Tunnel

BURNLEY A646

⑥

Stannally Stones

Bride Stones (farm)

Bride Stones Moor 1435' O.S. col S4501

Post Office

Lydgate

Stannally

①

Great Bride Stones

③

highest point of walk

KEB COTE

map extended to show approach from nearer Todmorden

Stoney Royd Lane

Whirlaw Stones form a well-defined edge high above

Whirlaw Stones

mast

②

ruin

Windy Harbour

BLACKSHAW HEAD

East Whirlaw

car park

mill

TODMORDEN CENTRE A646 (1 mile)

the superb stone causeway we travel. The map illustrates a higher alternative route above the stones, which are typical gritstone boulders interlaced with patches of heather.

36

WALK 9

6½ miles

BLAKE DEAN AND WALSHAW DEAN

from Widdop

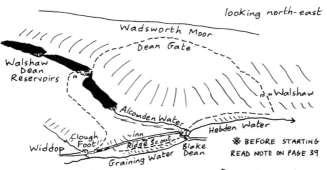

looking north-east

Wadsworth Moor

Dean Gate

Walshaw Dean Reservoirs

Walshaw

Alcomden Water

Hebden Water

Clough Foot

inn

Ridge Scout

Widdop

Blake Dean

Graining Water

※ BEFORE STARTING READ NOTE ON PAGE 39

Good paths traverse the open country around the head of Hardcastle Crags.

Start from the roadside parking area half a mile west of the Pack Horse inn on the Colne-Heptonstall road. (Grid ref: 946323).

THE WALK

From the lay-by follow the road south-east towards the Pack Horse, but beyond a lone house take a gate on the right giving access to a short-lived green way. At the end go left with a crumbling wall, then beyond a gate continue on with a wall on the left. When the path starts to descend to the right (becoming flagged) to the narrow valley bottom, keep straight on by the wall. A sketchy path skirts the pronounced drop, becoming clearer when the old wall parts company and the gritstone outcrops of Ridge Scout appear. In the vicinity of the boulders opt for the second right-hand fork, the path improving to run beneath the largest outcrops to a kissing gate.

Here the road is rejoined at a hairpin bend: go down to the bridge and take a drive on the left, leaving it at the first opportunity at a small gate to drop down to a wooden footbridge over Alcomden Water. Take the path climbing away, and when a broad green track is crossed, turn right along it. From a stile at the end a narrower path runs delightfully through trees to a lonely house, where a broad drive takes

37

over to head into the deeper woods at the head of Hebden Dale, better known as Hardcastle Crags.

After about 10 minutes a crossroads with narrower paths is reached, just before an inflowing beck on the left. Turn left up the narrow path through a gateway in an old wall, and steeply up to the top of the woods. At the wall go left to a small gate, and rise directly up the field to the impressive frontage of Walshaw shooting lodge. A little to its right a small enclosure is entered by a gate and left by a stile. The enclosed track rising directly from the top end of the yard is our route, but first read the note opposite.

On heading up the track, be ready to leave it as soon as it turns sharp left to New Cote Farm, by branching off up the untidy little tract of land. Head up to a gate in the angle of a short length of fence, then rise up the field-side on a track which improves shortly after becoming enclosed. On debouching onto the moor head straight up the narrow path, which breasts a high shoulder of Wadsworth Moor before dropping towards the reservoirs of Walshaw Dean. At a brace of shooting boxes the shooters' track is joined and followed down to the left.

Beyond a stile the Pennine Way is joined at the end of the middle reservoir's dam, which is then crossed. Turning left at the end, the reservoir road is followed back to the start, avoiding all forks to the left. At a bend just before the road a stile on the left cuts out a small corner to gain the lay-by.

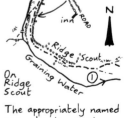

Widdop (6)

Clough Foot

COLNE

Pennine Way

✳

start 917'

The causey leads down to a charming watersmeet, worth a detour.

N

inn

ROAD

Ridge Scout

Graining Water

(1)

On Ridge Scout

The appropriately named inn stands astride an important pack route. Boots must be removed!

IMPORTANT: The path from Walshaw over Dean Gate to the foot of Walshaw Dean Middle Reservoir is a permissive path on Savile Estate land, and may be closed on certain days in the grouse shooting season and times of high fire risk. On such occasions a red flag is flown at the start of the path. A good alternative route, avoiding retracing steps, is to turn left at Walshaw, where a broad track runs unerringly to rejoin the main route near the walk's conclusion. Its two junctions are marked thus ▓ on the map.

⑤ Walshaw Dean Middle Reservoir

From the middle reservoir the Pennine Way climbs over the moor to enter 'Brontëland' at the ruin of Withins.

Walshaw Dean Lower Reservoir

shooting boxes

Wadsworth Moor

④ 1380'
↑ brow of hill

Dean Gate

N

The trio of reservoirs occupying most of the floor of Walshaw Dean was begun in 1900, but only fully completed in 1913 after solving problems with leakages. A steam powered railway was constructed to transport materials to the site, which at its peak employed over 500 men. A mighty wooden bridge carried the line 100 feet above Hebden Water in Blake Dean, and the 5 base pillars will be seen from the path, where the well-defined course of the line is also clearly discernable. Along with the workers' shanty town, one can easily visualise a 'wild west' scene.

Burial ground and site of Blake Dean Baptist Chapel (1802)

Alcomden Water

Immediately on entering the woods a spritely series of cascades descend from the left.

ROAD

ROAD

Blake Dean

bridge pillars

Hebden Water

New Cote Farm

③

⑤ Walshaw

Blake Dean is the archetypal 'beauty spot', a colourful watersmeet with grassy banks and green islands beneath steep bracken and gritstone studded slopes.

Walk 6 explores downstream

WALK 10

4 miles

| REDDYSHORE SCOUT AND ALLESCHOLES |

from Walsden

looking west

Reddyshore Scout

Allescholes

Summit Tunnel

Warland

Rochdale Canal

Walsden

Superb walking on green tracks through the impressive surrounds of the Walsden gorge. Quite a history trail, as well.

Start from the south end of the village by the Waggon and Horses inn. Various off-road parking places.

| THE WALK |

Leave Walsden by taking the Rochdale road (A6033) and turning up an enclosed path by the Waggon and Horses. At the top go right up the surfaced Allescholes farm road. Initially steep, with a hairpin bend, it soon eases to run up past the neighbouring Allescholes farms and along to a very sudden demise at a gate onto moorland.

A splendid level track heads away, passing by the Allescholes milestone high above the Summit Tunnel's course, and the narrow valley bottom below. At a gate between two pylons the way becomes enclosed, running dramatically atop the crest of Reddyshore Scout. The track continues unfailingly to drop eventually to the Calderbrook road.

Turn left down the road to a boundary sign and air shaft, then take a gate on the left to follow a green path heading back to Reddyshore Scout. This one however is to run beneath the cliffs, parallel with our outward leg. After a stile below the pylon it begins a steady descent past two more air shafts. On nearing the valley road a final air shaft is passed and a drive joined: cross straight over and down a nice cobbled snicket onto the main road.

Cross over and go left to steps joining Bottomley Road to gain access to the Rochdale Canal at Bottomley Lock. Go left on the towpath, leaving it after Lightbank Lock on a fieldpath doubling back to cross the railway line and a tiny beck back up to the road. Turn right for a quick return to the start.

Walsden is Todmorden's southerly 'suburb', occupying the narrow valley floor of little seen Walsden Water for some considerable length. South of the village, and for all our upland route, the railway burrows through the infamous Summit Tunnel, opened in 1840 and the scene of a dramatic fire in 1984. Its many air shafts are shown thus •

TODMORDEN A6033

Walsden

The outward route traces Reddyshore Scout Gate, a centuries-old packhorse route still in fine condition. The Allescholes Milestone is an outstanding specimen of some age, dramatically perched on the hilltop, and it bears the (very direct) distances to Todmorden, Rochdale, Burnley and Halifax.

The view south-east from the Scout includes Chelburn Reservoirs (built to serve the canal, one now dry) backed by Blackstone Edge.

Allescholes Milestone

Lightbank Lock

Rochdale Canal

lock ← see also Walk 4

Lower Allescholes

Bottomley Lock

Higher Allescholes

ROAD

① ③

Moor Hey

Allescholes Milestone

The Bird i'th' Hand inn at Warland is seen in true 'birds-eye' fashion from both paths above.

'link path'

pylons

950'

highest point

Reddyshore Scout

Reddyshore Scout

Owler Clough

Steanor Bottom Toll House is a 6-sided building astride a turnpike junction, with its list of charges admirably preserved.

LITTLEBOROUGH ROAD A6033

CALDERBROOK

②

Owler Clough, a charming series of cascades immediately above the road, marks the county boundary. Note the old stone (Todmorden/Littleborough) set in the wall.

41

WALK 11 | CRIMSWORTH DEAN AND LIMER'S GATE |

6 miles   from Midgehole

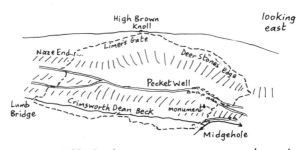

looking
east

High Brown
Knoll

Limers Gate

Naze End

Deer Stones Edge

Pecket Well

Crimsworth Dean Beck

Lumb
Bridge

monument

Midgehole

After a stiff start, an easy walk ensues to combine superb woodland and beck scenery with a bracing moorland ramble.

Use the National Trust car park at Midgehole. This (with overflow facilities) is the main car park for Hardcastle Crags, signposted off the Keighley road out of Hebden Bridge.

| THE WALK |

From the car park recross the bridge and take a narrow way climbing behind the toilets. Behind a solitary house bear left and continue climbing on a stony track between crumbling walls. As height is gained the towering Wadsworth war memorial may be seen high up to the left, and can easily be visited by branching off at some old steps from where a narrow path rises steeply left. A stile gives access to the small pasture containing the monument. From it retrace steps to the main path which has levelled out to cross a beck before meeting a similar path to rise steeply left onto the A6033 at Pecket Well.

Cross straight over the Hebden Bridge-Keighley road and up a short-lived path onto a wide back road, turning right along it. After a minute or two leave this road by the surfaced Shaw Croft Hill road up to the left: it ends at some houses but a walled track takes over, rising half-left. At a rough, open area either rise gradually (wet here) or double back steeply up onto a broad level track. Go left a short

The falls, Lumb Hole

Wadsworth War Memorial, looking to Stoodley Pike and Heptonstall

distance then strike sharp right up another walled track. At the top it emerges onto open moorland.

On the moor opt for the broad track rising half-right, but leave it within a minute by the higher of two long abandoned sunken tracks rising to the left. After levelling out it fades before meeting a level track at a wall corner. After a few yards with the wall it turns to rise across the moor, forking into two more sunken ways which merge on High Brown Knoll. clearly discernable Deer Stones Edge. A decent path runs northwards along this largely grassy edge, fading just beyond a substantial cairn to the right. Continue along the edge a little further before locating another reasonable grass path which swings across to the right before rising directly to the Ordnance column on High Brown Knoll.

A cairned path now strikes north-west above the modest Summer Rake Edge, remaining fairly clear to emerge at Naze End, with the A6033 just below. Descend to it and go left a few yards towards a canine cattle-grid: here bear off to the right, a narrow path being found in a damp section to drop straight down to a wall parallel to the road. A few yards to the right a small gate is the key to a wet, narrow path, descending enclosed to a quiet road.

Turn right past farm buildings and from a gate on the left an enclosed path descends the field-side to Crimsworth Dean Beck, turning right at the bottom to Lumb Bridge and Lumb Hole waterfall. Cross the bridge and head downstream, but as the main path climbs away, go left through a gateway on a narrower path.

Remaining parallel with the beck, the path contours through the encroaching bracken of several pastures, eventually encountering a stile and a humble dwelling before reaching a gate into the

Lumb Bridge
Lumb Hole
falls
Lumb Lane (a gem)
Crimsworth Dean Beck
⑤
Weet Ing Bridge
Hebden Water
HEBDEN BRIDGE
Wadsworth War Memorial
Midgehole (see also Walk 6)

The path downstream of Lumb Bridge is a joy to tread, with some splendid woodland opposite.

Wadsworth is the parish for Pecket Well, Old Town and Chiserley.

N

National Trust woods. From it a track rises to meet the main drive which descends unfailingly to the starting point, but a more interesting variation ignores the gate in favour of a wall-gap to its left, descending across the field to a stile into the woods.

A path runs down to a stone arched bridge which is not crossed, continuing instead on the same bank, rising a little then running along towards a gate into a field. One hundred yards before it however, rise half-right (junction sketchy) to join the main drive. This is now followed down to the left all the way back to Midgehole.

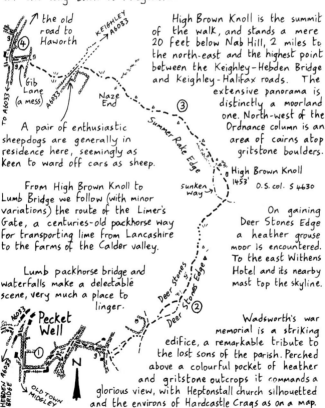

High Brown Knoll is the summit of the walk, and stands a mere 20 feet below Nab Hill, 2 miles to the north-east and the highest point between the Keighley–Hebden Bridge and Keighley–Halifax roads. The extensive panorama is distinctly a moorland one. North-west of the Ordnance column is an area of cairns atop gritstone boulders.

High Brown Knoll 1453'   O.S. col. S 4630

A pair of enthusiastic sheepdogs are generally in residence here, seemingly as keen to ward off cars as sheep.

From High Brown Knoll to Lumb Bridge we follow (with minor variations) the route of the Limer's Gate, a centuries-old packhorse way for transporting lime from Lancashire to the farms of the Calder valley.

On gaining Deer Stones Edge a heather grouse moor is encountered. To the east Withens Hotel and its nearby mast top the skyline.

Lumb packhorse bridge and waterfalls make a delectable scene, very much a place to linger.

Wadsworth's war memorial is a striking edifice, a remarkable tribute to the lost sons of the parish. Perched above a colourful pocket of heather and gritstone outcrops it commands a glorious view, with Heptonstall church silhouetted and the environs of Hardcastle Crags as on a map.

45

WALK 12

5¾ miles

An intimate exploration of the valley, returning along quiet roads and green lanes.

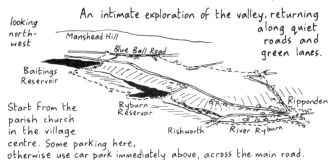

looking north-west

Start from the parish church in the village centre. Some parking here, otherwise use car park immediately above, across the main road.

THE WALK

From the church do not cross either of the bridges, but pass between the houses at Bridge End and *underneath* the road bridge over the Ryburn. A drive then heads upstream, through the park to some houses and a small industrial estate. Here remain on the riverbank path, rising briefly above the Ryburn at some steps by a footbridge, to descend through the trees to the river and on to its confluence with Booth Dean Beck.

Here cross the inflowing beck and up onto the main road, using that to cross the Ryburn itself before departing left immediately on Bar Lane, parallel with the river. It runs upstream to an eventual demise at a mill, a cobbled road then taking over at an underpass below the mill. At a hairpin bend leave to go round the left of a garage, where a footpath is found with a mill pond below and Ryburn dam spectacularly in front. At a stile a choice presents itself: either turn down the path to the valley floor and up the opposite bank (path obvious), or take the easier route up to the right, emerging at the dam's north end before proceeding to cross it.

At the far end take the track right, above the water's edge to reach a footbridge over the head of the reservoir's southern arm. A path climbs through trees into a field, then rises by a wall to become enclosed before arriving at a farm. Go right of the buildings (a trifle messy here) and directly up the field behind, rising in a straight line before levelling out to run along to a stile. Continue along this pleasant crest, becoming enclosed again at the end, then leave by a small gate to gain access to the Withins-like ruin just down to the right.

From the wall corner by the ruin follow the level wall in the direction of Baitings Reservoir, soon becoming enclosed to reach a large barn. At a smaller barn opposite leave the track by a gate to cross two fields to Higher Wormald Farm. Here turn right down a track to the dam of Baitings Reservoir, crossing it to join the A58 at a well-sited hostelry. A sketchy path climbs the rough pasture behind it to a parallel road with an even more prominent white-walled inn, the Blue Ball.

Now turn right along the quiet, level road (avoiding lesser turns) for a good threequarters of a mile, then just beyond a T-junction go right on a broad, walled track bound for London Spring farm. Continue straight past it and along to another road, going left only a few yards before branching to the right down another walled track. At the far end cross straight over a road, behind a house, over a second road and on again, where a contrastingly narrow green way descends between walls onto a narrow lane.

This is Royd Lane, and it leads steeply and rapidly down into the centre of Ripponden, and the car park. For the parish church cross straight over the main road and down a short lane to the Bridge inn and the packhorse bridge.

Ripponden

Blue Ball   Baitings   New Inn

West of the reservoir are only lonely moors

LITTLEBOROUGH A58

Baitings Reservoir

completed 1956

Higher Wormald

900'

③ R. Ryburn

car park

inn

inn 950'

RIPPONDEN A58

New House (ruin)

New Barn has some rare breeds (a reminder to keep dogs on leads).

Ryburn Reservoir (1933)

New Barn

② Ryburn Reservoir

WC

Note the quaint fire appliance in its own garage at the mill.

paper mill

trout farm

Ryburn's valley has no shortage of trees!

River Ryburn

Both concrete dams could rapidly induce vertigo, the curiously curved one at Baitings having unusually low walls (hold on to your false teeth if brave enough to peer over it). Beneath Ryburn's dam it is interesting to compare man's 'progress' in methods of conserving water; the splendid old mill pond being overshadowed by the hundred foot high dam.

Ripponden is a busy little village, its old centre being a conservation area. Here is St. Bartholomew's church, its spire reaching to the heavens, a restored packhorse bridge, and the white-walled and equally old Bridge inn. A farm museum can be found only yards along the road.

The neighbouring hostelries at Baitings both display interesting appendages, one a large sundial, the other a short verse.

The return walk has good views over to Norland Moor and down the Ryburn to Sowerby Bridge, where it meets the Calder.

Blue Ball Road

④ RIPPONDEN

955' SOYLAND

London Spring

Green Lane

Low Cote.

Cote Road

COTTON STONES

SOYLAND

⑤ inn

hen huts

① RISHWORTH A672 ← ROAD

Here a path rises to a redundant bridge over the defunct railway from Sowerby Bridge to Rishworth.

weir

→ Z

Royd Lane

Sunny Bank

SOYLAND

weir ROAD

Although the M62 motorway is not actually seen, its proximity is likely to be all too evident.

Ripponden

inn

GREETLAND B6113 ←

SOWERBY BRIDGE A58

WALK 13

5¾ miles

JUMBLE HOLE CLOUGH AND GREAT ROCK

from Lobb Mill

Start from the Lobb Mill picnic site/car park 1½ miles east of Todmorden centre on the Hebden Bridge road.

looking north-west

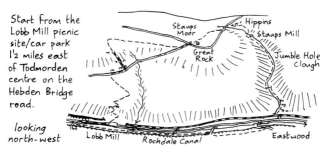

A labrynth of hillside tracks and lanes, and a simple towpath trod sandwich the highlight of the walk, a descent of the fascinating Jumble Hole Clough.

THE WALK

Leave the car park by the path at its eastern end, rising across the breast of this pocket of open country. As it zig-zags up avoid any lesser forks and at the top the wide path becomes enclosed to approach a group of buildings. Pass between them and on to a T-junction of walled tracks, then turn left and remain on the same track to eventually rise up to a road.

Turn right along the road for a couple of minutes and then take a private-looking drive up to the left between two houses. It climbs steeply until turning sharply left at a lone dwelling: here go straight up a partly-overgrown way which within a few yards meets a good path. Turn right along it, immediately through a gapstile and across to a beck. Less distinctly it passes above the confines of a renovated farm to meet a sunken way on the other side. Rising gently between long-collapsed walls, it doubles back a little before levelling out to run as a splendid green track along a field bottom. At the far end it becomes enclosed to emerge onto a lane.

Head up the lane to a junction and then right to the prominent Great Rock on the very roadside. Here take an enclosed track to its left. On debouching onto Staups

Moor it turns to descend by a wall, crossing a stile into a field to drop steeply onto a road. Cross Hippins Bridge to turn immediately right on an access track: when it swings sharply left take a kissing-gate in front and follow the wall away. A stile in it marks the point to branch off right, a path soon materialising to descend stone steps to a footbridge across the beck.

The ruin of Staups Mill is passed and as the path rises, take a left fork to remain parallel with but high above the beck. After passing with care above a substantial crag the path descends to cross two field-bottoms, returning into the woods to be absorbed into a farm drive. Just below an old mill pond it doubles back to cross the beck, then clings to its other bank to arrive at the buildings at Jumble Hole.

At the railway underpass turn right on a drive parallel with the line, continuing into the trees until a footbridge crosses the railway. Dropping to the main road go right only a few yards before escaping over a river bridge alongside a mill. Continue on to also cross a canal bridge, then turn immediately right onto a footpath which runs delightfully through the wood above the canal bank.

Eventually the canal is rejoined at the next bridge, which is crossed to follow the towpath for a mile to the lock and road bridge at Lobb Mill. Turn right to rejoin the main road by a viaduct and right again to return to the starting point.

Staups Mill

Great Rock

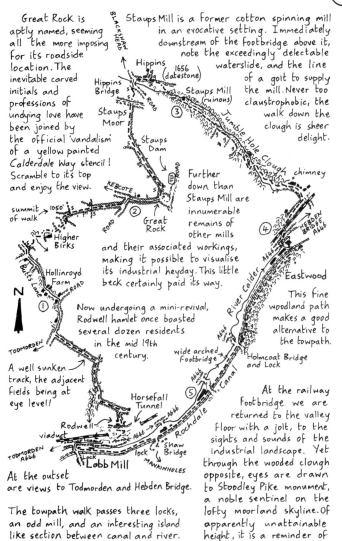

Great Rock is aptly named, seeming all the more imposing for its roadside location. The inevitable carved initials and professions of undying love have been joined by the official vandalism of a yellow painted Calderdale Way stencil! Scramble to it's top and enjoy the view.

Staups Mill is a former cotton spinning mill in an evocative setting. Immediately downstream of the footbridge above it, note the exceedingly delectable waterslide, and the line of a goit to supply the mill. Never too claustrophobic, the walk down the clough is sheer delight.

Further down than Staups Mill are innumerable remains of other mills and their associated workings, making it possible to visualise its industrial heyday. This little beck certainly paid its way.

Now undergoing a mini-revival, Rodwell hamlet once boasted several dozen residents in the mid 19th century.

A well sunken track, the adjacent fields being at eye level!

At the outset are views to Todmorden and Hebden Bridge.

The towpath walk passes three locks, an odd mill, and an interesting island like section between canal and river. Yes, that was the Calder.

This fine woodland path makes a good alternative to the towpath.

At the railway footbridge we are returned to the valley floor with a jolt, to the sights and sounds of the industrial landscape. Yet through the wooded clough opposite, eyes are drawn to Stoodley Pike monument, a noble sentinel on the lofty moorland skyline. Of apparently unattainable height, it is a reminder of Calderdale's rich character.

Map labels: BLACKSHAW HEAD, Hippins, 1656 (datestone), Hippins Bridge, Staups Mill (ruins), Hippins Road, Staups Moor, Staups Dam, KEBCOTE, ROAD, ③, Tumble Hole Clough, chimney, summit of walk, 1050', ②, Great Rock, ROAD, Higher Birks, Butts Lane, Hollinroyd Farm, ROAD, ①, N, TODMORDEN, HEBDEN BRIDGE A646, ④, Eastwood, River Calder, A646, wide arched Footbridge, A646, Holmcoat Bridge and Lock, Rochdale Canal, ⑤, Horsefall Tunnel, A646, Rodwell, viaduct, TODMORDEN A646, Shaw Bridge, lock, MANKINHOLES, LOCK, Lobb Mill

WALK 14

7 miles

| BELL HOUSE MOOR AND WITHENS CLOUGH |

From Cragg Vale

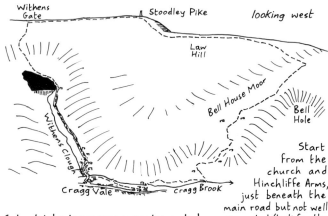

looking west

Splendid beck scenery precedes a climb to breezy moorland. Wonderful views and a host of fine features more than compensate for several damp moments. Wait for a dry spell!

Start from the church and Hinchliffe Arms, just beneath the main road but not well signposted (look for the church tower). Parking space opposite the inn. Grid ref: 999232.

| THE WALK |

   From the bridge by the inn take the private road on the church side of Cragg Brook, soon ending at a yard. Cross to a narrow gate between the houses from where a green path runs downstream to a bridge. Remaining on this bank continue on the broad track rising above the beck, past houses and along towards the road. Just before the road, however, fork left at the last house, through a private-looking yard and down a concrete track to another bridge.
   This time cross the beck and turn right up a track, soon levelling out to run high above the wooded beck. When the left-hand wall disappears we are immersed in the wood: within yards fork right, down towards the beck, and from a gate cross two narrow pastures to emerge onto a drive. Go down it to a bridge, but then strike sharply left up a few steps, keeping with the wall to rise past a house into trees.

On leaving the trees follow a short, sunken way up the field, and when it ends continue up the wet pasture, passing left of a house to find a stile in the very corner at the top. Head right with a fence to another stile at the far end, to enter an unappealing enclosed way. At the top Higher Cragg farm is reached and a better track rises away. Above a bend take the left-hand of two gates from where the track rises by a wall: after a fence takes over cross a stile in it and head up again, soon being deflected right by the well sunken road to Bell House, visible across to the right. Remain with the sunken way to a stile onto Bell House Moor, and cross the wet corner to Bell House.

From the outside of Bell House's yard rise up to the left on a track to soon meet a stone causeway, and follow its course to the right. Unfortunately its surface never properly reappears after a squelchy section, but the path remains clear to contour round to the unmistakeable head of the mighty head of Bell Hole.

Leave the rim of Bell Hole by striking directly away over the moor, aiming for a highly conspicuous gate in the wall on the western skyline. Traces of a path are scant, but roughly half-way across a clear path marked by a series of upright stones is crossed at right-angles. Ironically our path now improves as we forsake it in favour of this clearer path rising up to the left. Soon a reliable guide appears in the shape of a ruinous barn, and as walls close in we are drawn unfailingly to Dick's Lane, the right-hand green way. The monument on Stoodley Pike now beckons and draws us along the length of the lane, turning right at the end to a gapstile from where the Pennine Way rises with ease up to the monument itself.

An easy mile of the Pennine Way now ensues as the well-defined escarpment to the south of the Pike is followed, eventually dropping a little through old quarries to a crossroads with a well-preserved paved way. Turn to the left along it, the flags not surviving too far but the path remaining clear to the watershed wall at Withens Gate.

On the other side of the stile there stands the squat Te Deum Stone, and heading away from it is the broad path beginning the descent to Withens Clough. When the accompanying wall ends, continue down the line of an old wall, and through a maze of sorry walls a direct and obvious drop is made to Withens Clough Reservoir. Turn left on the road to the dam, from where a surfaced road drops back to the start.

At Withens Gate

Stoodley Pike is a
famous landmark
with superb views
westwards across
Langfield Common
(see also Walk 16).
The spring east of
it bursts forth
into a trough
inscribed 'PUBLIC
SLAKE TROUGH'.

Te Deum Stone

Long Stoop

Dick's Lane is a broad green way with extensive panoramas
westward to the moors enclosing Todmorden, and northward
to the deep wooded confines of Jumble Hole Clough, Colden
Water and the upper reaches of Hardcastle Crags.
Heptonstall, with its church tower is prominent
on its green ridge between the latter two.
Old boundary stones share Dick's Lane.

The Te Deum
Stone's Latin
inscription is,
translated, 'We
praise thee O Lord!',
and being on the
summit of the
Mankinholes-Withens
track is likely to
have been used
for resting
coffins when
bound for
Heptonstall.

The neighbourhood
of Withens Gate is
a fascinating area. Here
the modern foot-travellers highway,
the Pennine Way, meets a centuries
old packhorse route known (like several
others) as the Long Causeway. A splendid
preserved section of flags can be seen going
down towards Mankinholes. Presiding
over this crossroads is the Long
Stoop, an old guidepost of
monumental stature.

Stoodley
Pike 1307'
monument

spring

Dick's Lane

Law Hill

L = Long
Stoop

Te Deum Stone

Withens
Gate
1208'

Calderdale
Way alternative

Withens
Clough
Reservoir

car
park

Withens
Clough Reservoir
appears ahead.

one of
several
relatively
unobtrusive grass
covered dams locally.

The reservoir was completed in 1891.

Approaching Bell Hole

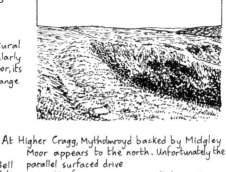

Bell Hole is a natural amphitheatre spectacularly scooped out of the moor, its hollow filled with a range of hardy old trees.

At Higher Cragg, Mytholmroyd backed by Midgley Moor appears to the north. Unfortunately the parallel surfaced drive below the farm seems to be 'out of bounds'.

Below Whams are views over the valley to Robin Hood's Rocks

Cragg Vale's claim to 'infamy' is as the home of the Yorkshire Coiners.
It is the most romantically recalled (though far from only) site of 18th century counterfeiting: the practice involved clipping gold from guineas to make inferior coins. At Bell House – unquestionably remote – lived the leader of the coiners, 'King David' Hartley. He was eventually hanged at York, and his grave can be seen at Heptonstall (walk 1).

Brief alternative along the surviving mill race

Cragg Brook is also known as the Elphin

Map labels: boundary stones; Erringden Moor; Bell Hole; Bell House Moor; Bell House; Keelham; Higher Cragg; Whams; N; MYTHOLMROYD B6138; Spa Laithe; Spa Bridge; Cragg Brook; Cragg Vale; ROAD; inn; Cragg Vale; Withens Clough; ↓ LITTLEBOROUGH B6138

Cragg Vale has bleak moorland beginnings but soon transforms into a richly-wooded deep valley before joining the Calder valley at Mytholmroyd. The first mile of the walk shadows Cragg Brook through fascinating terrain with numerous reminders of the mills it was made to serve. The sombre church is that of 'St. John in the Wilderness', while the adjacent inn displays 'coiners' memorabilia'.

WALK 15

5¼ miles

from Widdop

A trio of
moorland
waters linked
by clear and
very pleasant
paths and tracks.

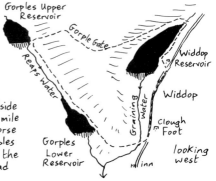

Start from the roadside
parking area half a mile
west of the Pack Horse
inn, where the Gorples
reservoir road leaves the
Heptonstall- Colne road
(Grid ref: 946323).

THE WALK

From the lay-by take the gate across the road and
head away along the reservoir road with its two concrete
strips. It leads first to the dam of Gorples Lower Reservoir, to
then continue alongside the water and its feeder Reaps Water.
Remain on it until arrival at the dam of the second sheet of
water, Gorples Upper Reservoir. Again ignore the track across
the dam, and instead cross the water catchment drain on the
right and take a thin path climbing directly up the slope of
Shuttleworth Moor. Initially steep, it soon eases to rise through the
various outcrops of this broad tongue to join a wide track.

This track is known as Gorple Gate and is followed to
the right, gently descending before dropping left rather steeply
to a sharp bend. Here take a narrower path to the left, again
dropping gradually with the remains of a wall. Below is Widdop
Reservoir, and just beyond its head drop right to a footbridge. A
few yards beyond it a wide track is joined and followed right.

Pass between a wall and a drain for a few yards then
cross the drain by a footbridge and head left again, infallibly
between the drain and the reservoir. When the trees disappear
a better track comes in, still by the shore until beyond an old
house it recrosses the drain and heads up to the road. Go right
on this largely unfenced moor road, past Clough Foot to the start.

The moorland Colne-Heptonstall road was an important trans- Pennine packhorse route three centuries ago, lime and cloth being major goods. Gorple Gate is another old way over the moors to Worsthorne in Lancashire.

Impressive and substantial rock formations here

Gorple Upper Res'r

1420' ← highest point

Gorple Gate

lectern guidepost

Shuttleworth Moor

Clattering Stones

sections of causey

ruin

③

COLNE →

ROAD

②

shooting box

Reaps Water

④

Widdop Reservoir

ROAD

The two Gorples reservoirs were completed in 1934.

Almost equalling their joint capacity is Widdop Reservoir, built over 50 years earlier. Materials reached the site by means of a 5½ mile long horse-drawn tramway from further down the valley. Some outstanding gritstone crags flank the reservoir to the north.

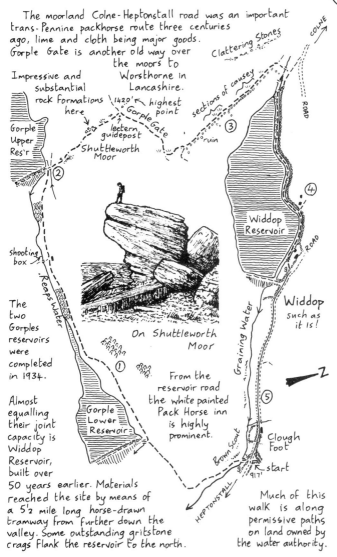

On Shuttleworth Moor

Gorple Lower Reservoir

①

From the reservoir road the white painted Pack Horse inn is highly prominent.

Graining Water

Widdop such as it is!

⑤

Z

Brown Scout

Clough Foot

HEPTONSTALL

917'

start

Much of this walk is along permissive paths on land owned by the water authority.

57

WALK 16

7 miles

| LANGFIELD EDGE AND STOODLEY PIKE |

from Lumbutts

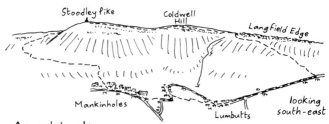

An exhilarating high-level march requiring a relatively small amount of effort.

There is ample parking in Lumbutts on the dead-end road to the Top Brink inn in the centre of the hamlet.

| THE WALK |

From the Top Brink descend either the enclosed path or the road by the old tower and head along the endlessly rising road for a long three-quarters of a mile as far as another hostelry, the Shepherds Rest. Here take a gate on the left and follow a good track climbing steadily across the moor. Avoiding a lesser fork left fairly early, the track forks again by some old workings: this time take the level left branch, which within a few yards proves itself to be the main path.

Now narrower but totally foolproof, the path rises imperceptibly as it nears the dark cliffs of Langfield Edge. Eventually this superbly engineered way gains the brooding rocks at their far end, then a path contours around the head of the clough below and doubles back across the far side. The path becomes sketchy before commencing a sunken descent, but our route avoids this loss of height by taking a thin path up to the right: it improves a little as it runs above a well-defined edge enhanced by a rash of boulders.

As the slope tails off so do the rocks, and the path heads more to the right, skirting the top of Coldwell Hill but running along towards a prominent cairn atop a rock platform. From here either join the unmistakeable course of

58

the Pennine Way yards to the right, or remain near the better defined 'edge' as long as possible. Either way it is the Pennine Way which soon takes us north, undulating a little at the Withens Gate path crossroads before rising through an old quarry and following the broad path along to the Stoodley Pike monument.

Leave the top with the Pennine Way as it strikes eastward, dropping to two neighbouring stiles and then down below Doe Stones. On encountering a sunken quarry track in a slight depression, with the farm ahead almost hidden, turn down it to descend to a wide track, and go left to a gate. This dead-level track contours beneath the Pike's steep slopes, and is vacated after almost a mile, over a stile in the accompanying fence just prior to the first farm buildings alongside (the monument is now directly above).

Almost immediately an access road is joined, leading down onto Lee Bottom Road. Turn left past the houses and at a sharp bend by the hospital at the far end, continue straight on up a narrow bridleway to emerge onto another road. Head up it, soon turning left to approach Mankinholes. Opposite the first building however turn down a paved lane to return unfailingly to the start at Lumbutts.

Langfield Edge and Lumbutts from Mankinholes

59

The monument on Stoodley Pike was erected in 1815 after victory over Napoleon, but later collapsed and was replaced by a new tower in 1856. It stands a mighty 120 feet above the moortop, and is the upper valley's most famous landmark. A dark, spiral staircase climbs forty steps to a viewing balcony: a pleasing feature of the extensive view is the way intervening slopes mask the industrialised valley floor.

The monument is in view from the outset, but frustratingly seems to keep its distance!

Mankinholes is an old weaving settlement largely by-passed by the 20th century. The great water troughs are a sign of its importance in packhorse days.

Langfield Edge bears old quarries and shapely rock formations, in stark contrast to the flat moors immediately above.

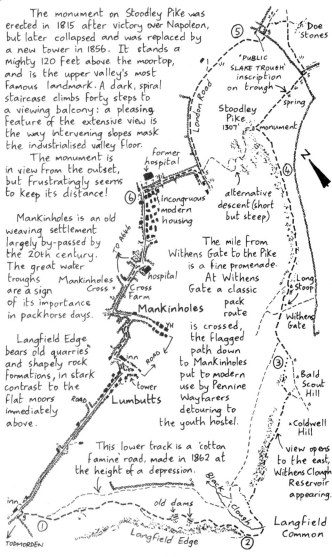

Doe Stones

(5)

'PUBLIC SLAKE TROUGH' inscription on trough

London Road

Stoodley Pike 1307' monument

spring

N

(4)

alternative descent (short but steep)

former hospital

(6)

incongruous modern housing

TO A646

hospital

Mankinholes Cross × Cross Farm

Mankinholes

YH

inn

ROAD

tower

ROAD Lumbutts

The mile from Withens Gate to the Pike is a fine promenade. At Withens Gate a classic pack route is crossed, the flagged path down to Mankinholes put to modern use by Pennine Wayfarers detouring to the youth hostel.

Long Stoop

Withens Gate

(3)

Bald Scout Hill

Coldwell Hill

view opens to the east, Withens Clough Reservoir appearing.

This lower track is a 'cotton famine' road, made in 1862 at the height of a depression.

old dams

Black Clough

inn

(1)

TODMORDEN

Langfield Edge

(2)

Langfield Common

The water wheel tower, Lumbutts

The tower completely dominates the little settlement of Lumbutts, which nestles in a hollow below Mankinholes. This immense structure once contained three vertically arranged wheels, each fed from above as well as independently. It served a cotton mill that once stood here.

Immediately above the tower is Lee Dam, scene of an annual New Year 'dip'.

Mankinholes

LOG OF THE WALKS

These two pages provide an opportunity to maintain a permanent record of the walks completed.

WALK	DATE	TIME Start	Finish	WEATHER	COMMENTS
1					
2					
3					
4					
5					
6					
7					
8					

WALK	DATE	TIME Start	Finish	WEATHER		COMMENTS	
9							
10							
11							
12							
13							
14							
15							
16							

KEY TO THE MAP SYMBOLS

direction of north

scale
2½ inches = 1 mile

Route — clear — sketchy — no visible path

Route on public road — unenclosed — wall — fence/hedge

River/beck — bridge

Marsh

Peat grough

Crags

Trees

Loose rocks/ scree

Cairns
summit   other

Canal

Buildings

Church

Abbreviations
c = cattle grid
s = stile
g = gate

Miles from start
③

Railway line

THE COUNTRY CODE

Respect the life and work of the countryside
Protect wildlife, plants and trees
Keep to public paths across farmland
Safeguard water supplies
Go carefully on country roads
Keep dogs under control - preferably on a lead
Guard against all risks of fire
Fasten all gates
Leave no litter - take it with you
Make no unnecessary noise
Leave livestock, crops and machinery alone
Use gates and stiles to cross fences, hedges and walls

Remember that - with a few exceptions - even the open moors
are privately owned, and access is only along the paths